DOT-TO-DOT

Anna Pomaska

DOVER PUBLICATIONS, INC.
Mineola, New York

Bibliographical Note

Dot-to-Dot, first published in 2005, is a republication of the work
first published by Dover Publications, Inc., in 1997.

International Standard Book Number

ISBN-13: 978-0-486-44700-1
ISBN-10: 0-486-44700-6

Manufactured in the United States by LSC Communications
44700612   2017
www.doverpublications.com

The cat is driving on with speed,
Delivering to those in need.

6

7

8

3

2

1

5

4

This aids the farmer every day;
It helps him cut and haul the hay.

2

This is a thing we build from sand;
We mold it into shape by hand.

My home I carry on my back,
So when I roam I never pack.

4

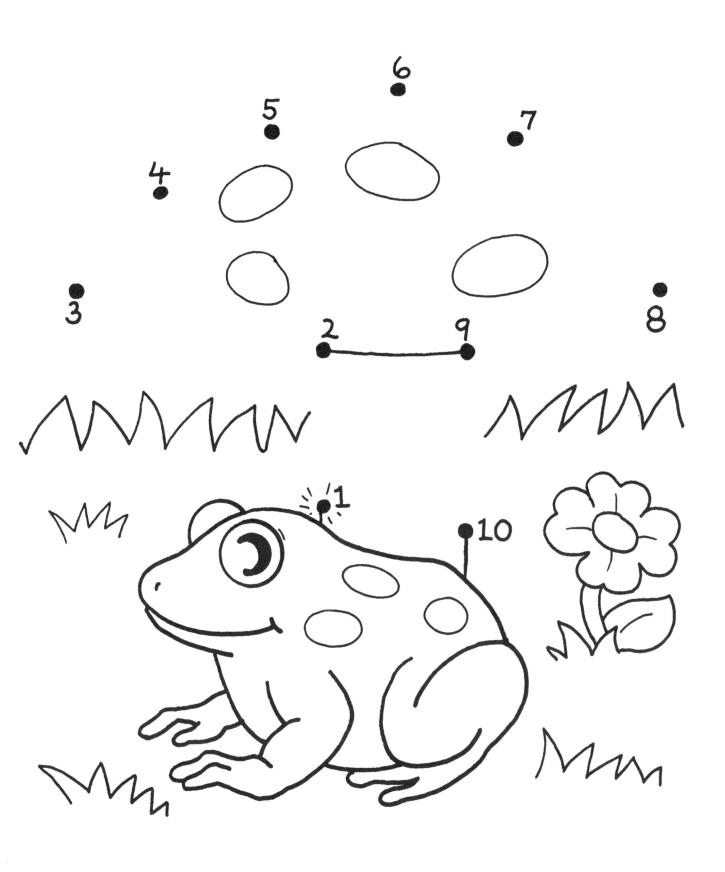

This toad is sitting on the ground.
What shelters him as he looks 'round?

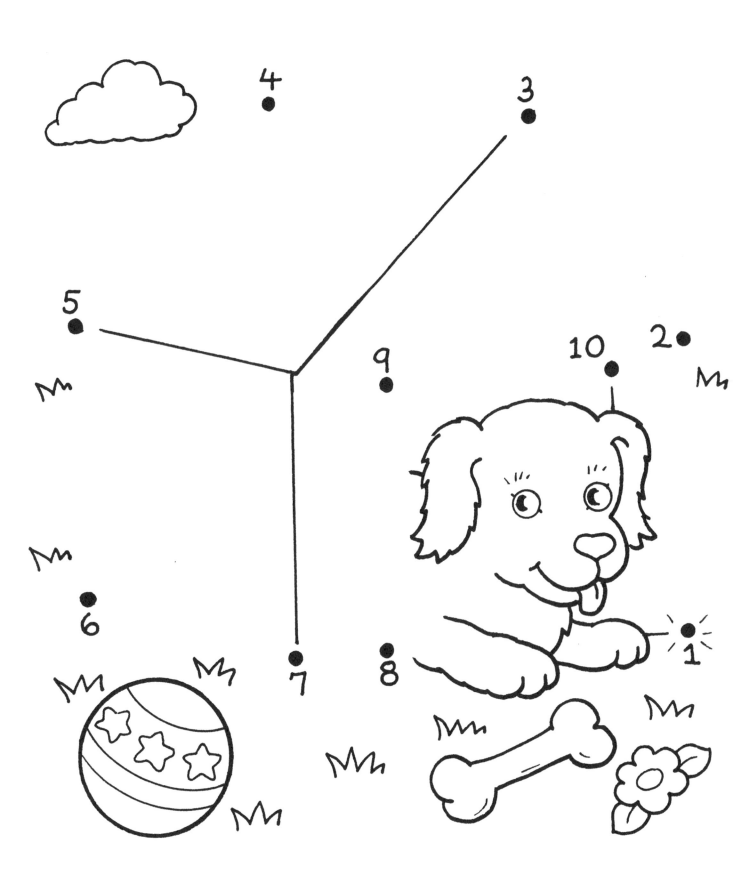

This place is Fido's very own;
It's where he chews upon his bone.

This creature loves the sea and fish;
To swim in oceans is her wish.

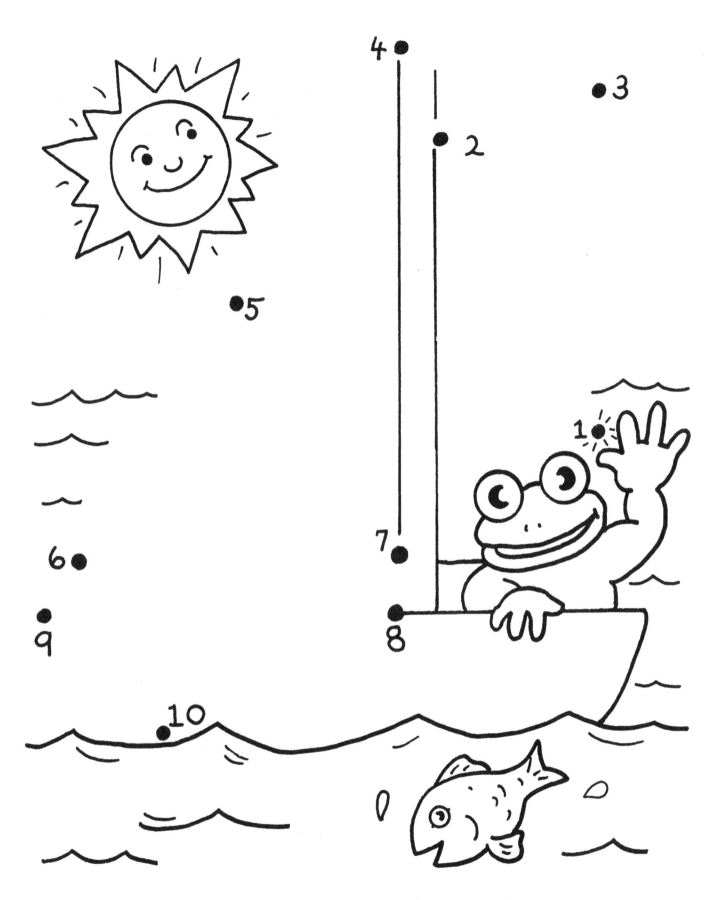

The frog is waving with great glee.
What lets him sail upon the sea?

The bears look up into the night,
And what they see is big and bright.

With this we fly so high in space;
We look the moon right in the face!

This bird, of swimming very fond,
Just quacks and swims on this small pond.

I breathe in water, swimming free,
So I am found beneath the sea.

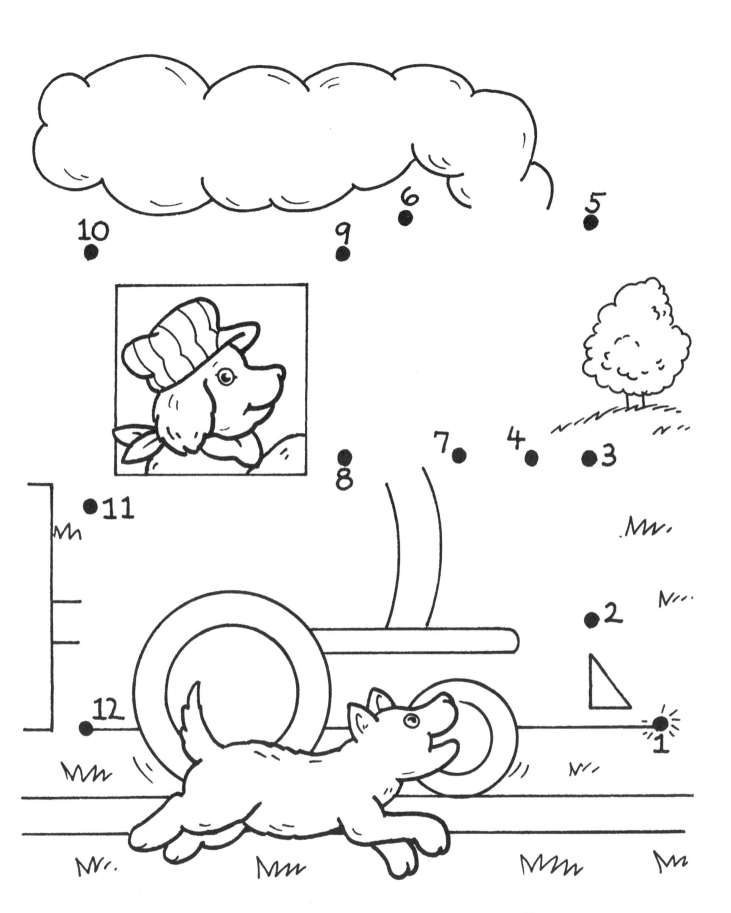

I smoke and ride along a rail,
And barking dogs give me a hail.

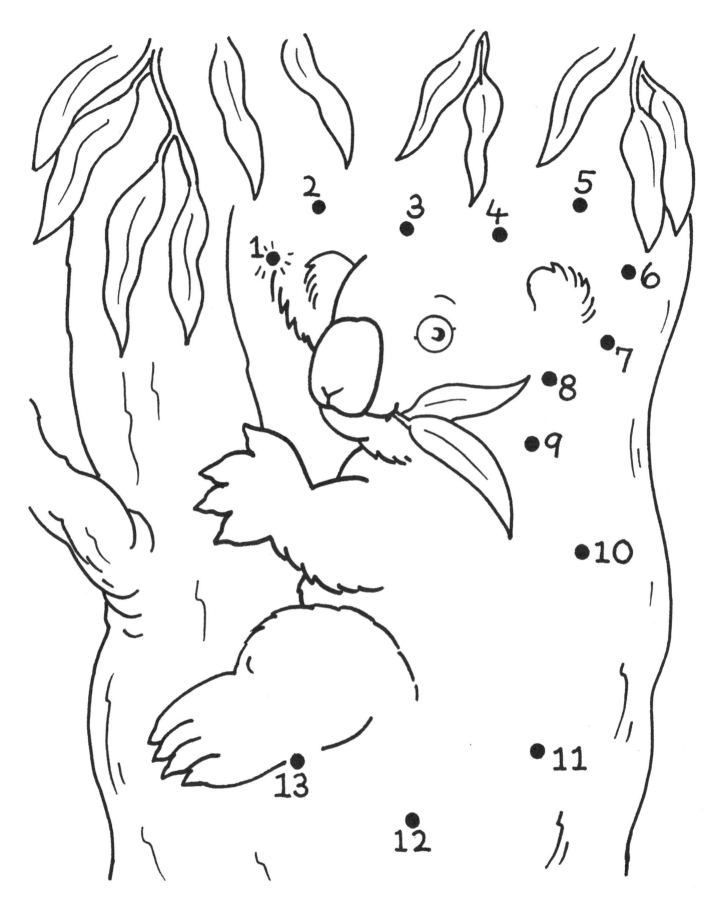

To munch on leaves I'm always ready;
Though not a bear, I look like Teddy.

This bird lives in the ice and cold,
Can't fly, but in the sea is bold.

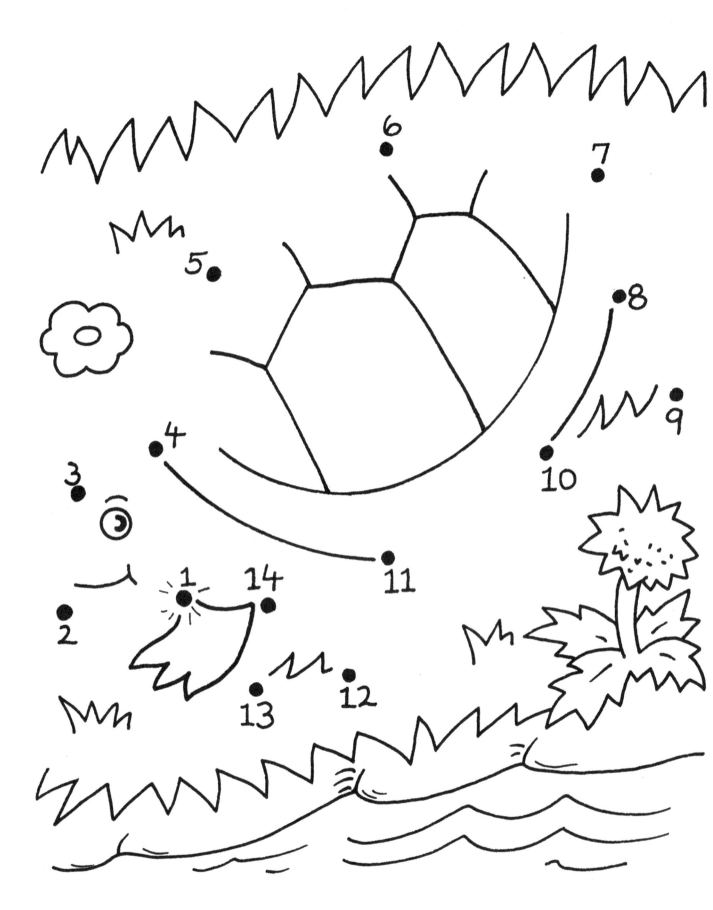

My walking is considered slow;
My shell protects me from my foe.

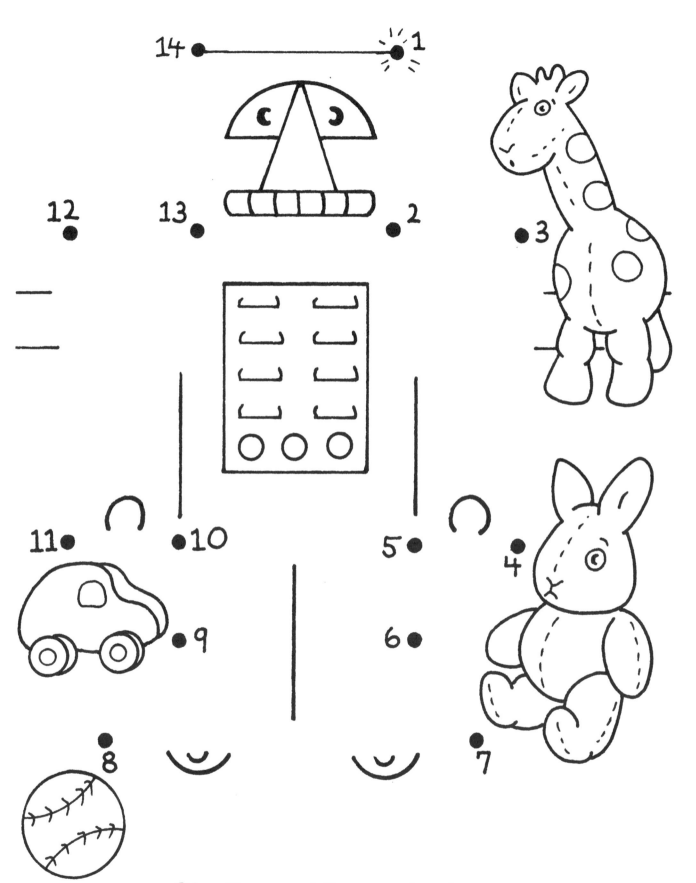

14 ● 1
12
13 ● 2
● 3
11 ● ● 10
5 ● ● 4
● 9
6 ●
● 8
● 7

Giraffe and Bunny try to see
What kind of creature this can be.

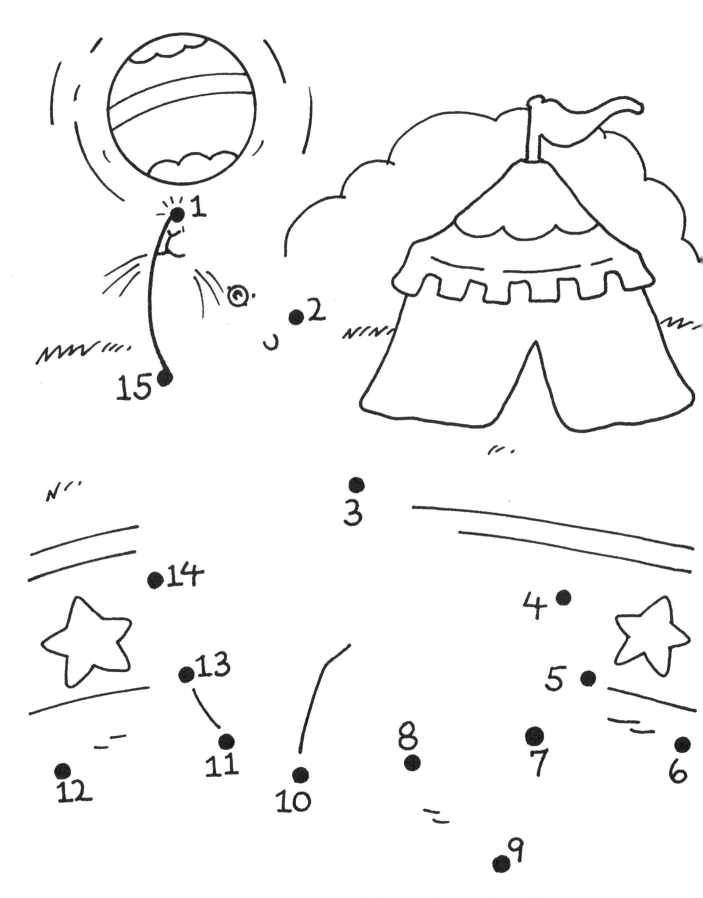

1

15

2

3

14

13

11

12

10

8

7

5

4

6

9

On my nose I juggle a ball,
And never ever let it fall!

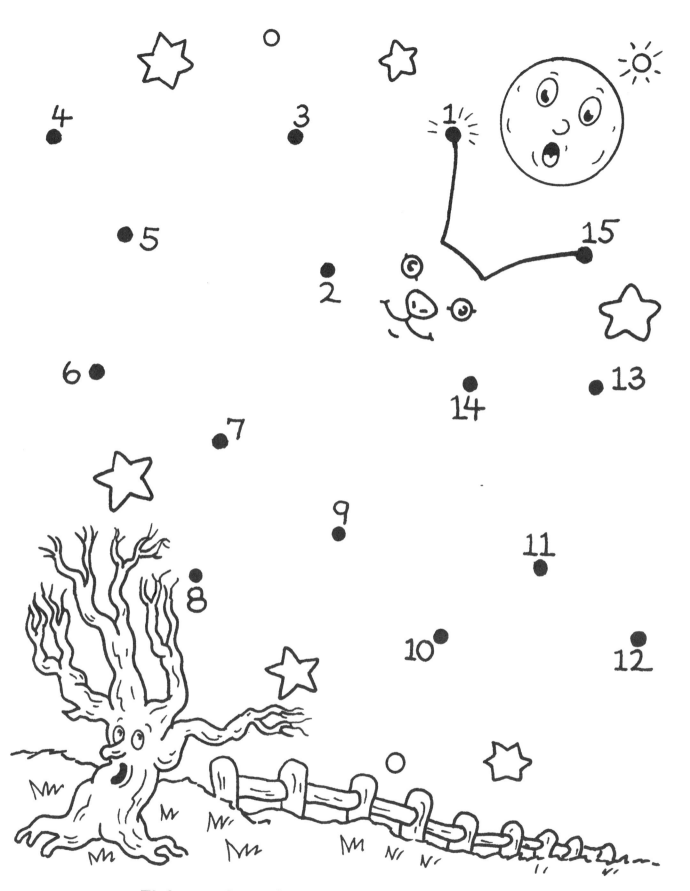

This animal comes out at night;
When flying he can cause a fright.

19

What is Teddy riding on?
Connect the dots before he's gone!

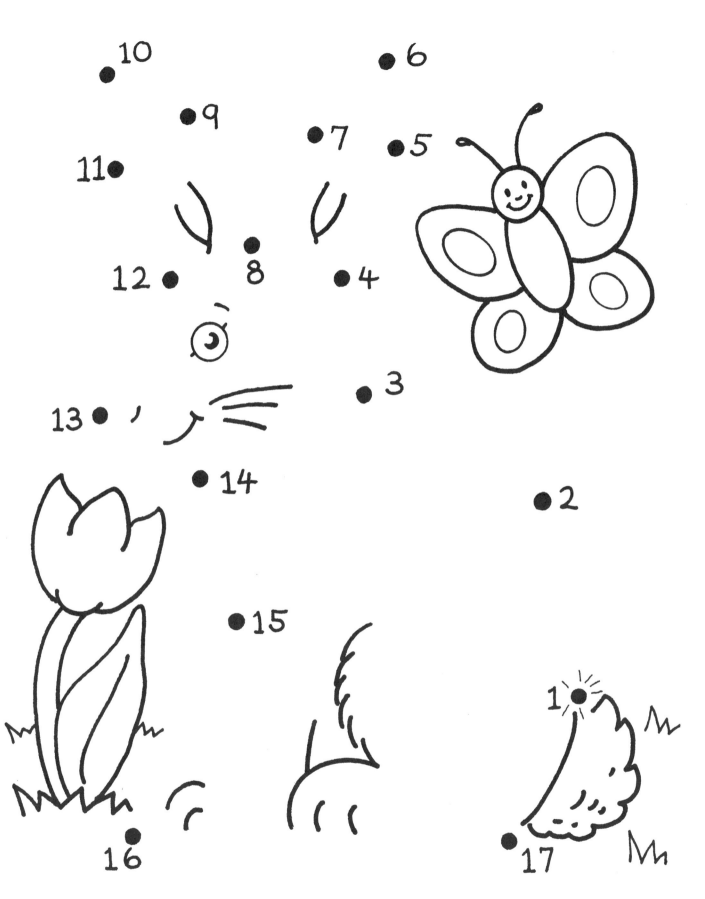

Who has long ears and likes to hop?
Connect every dot before you stop!

This lets the puppy fly so high
Among the birdies in the sky.

The water that's inside this thing
Makes garden flowers grow in spring.

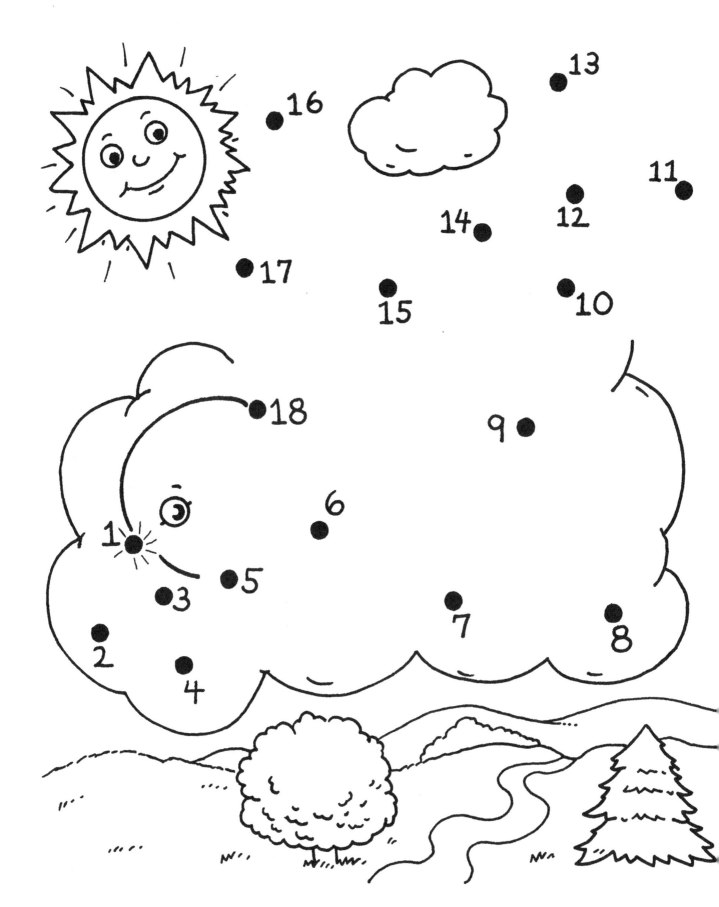

I flap my wings and off I go,
Leaving the streams and trees below.

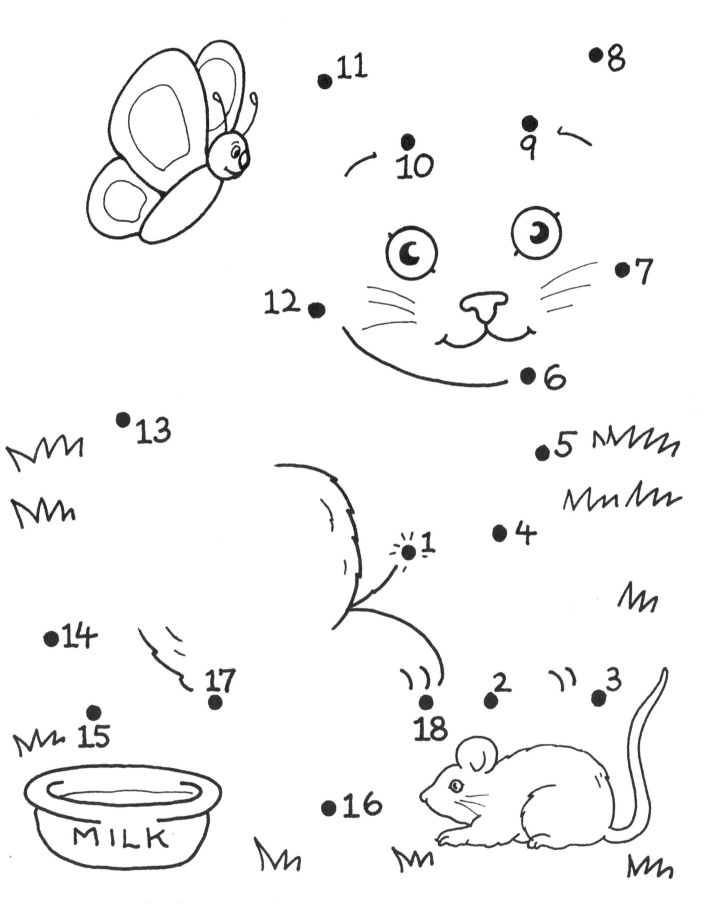

I chase mice and I lap up milk,
And keep my fur as smooth as silk.

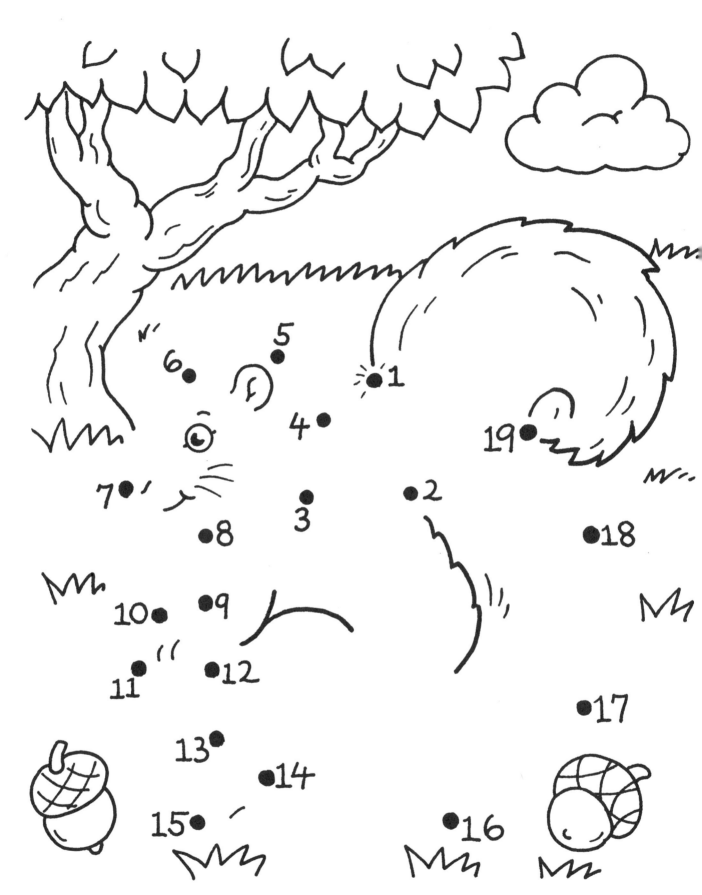

My bushy tail's a help to me
When jumping high from tree to tree.

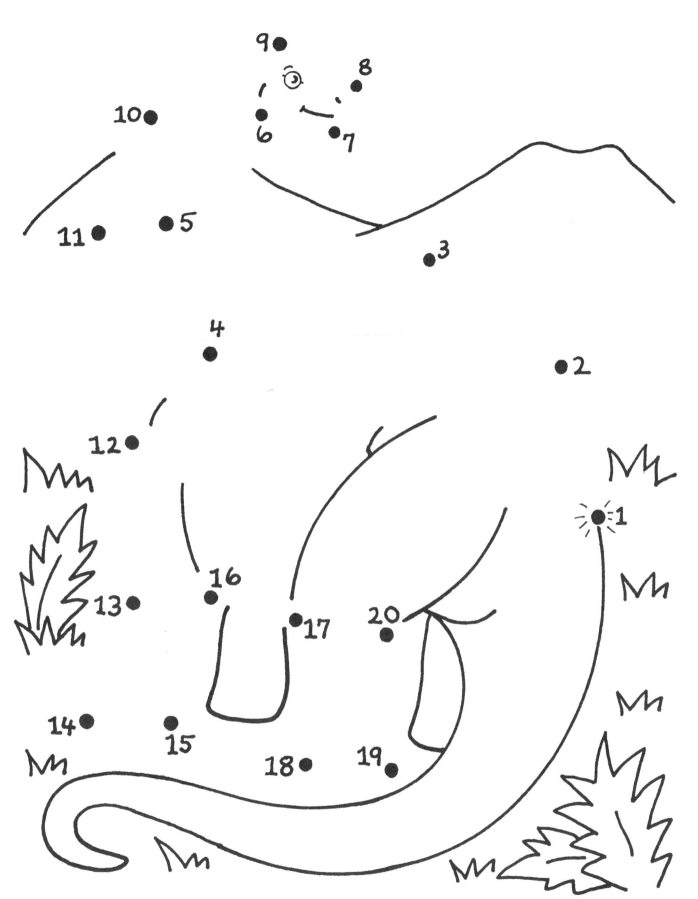

This creature once was huge and great,
But long ago it met its fate.

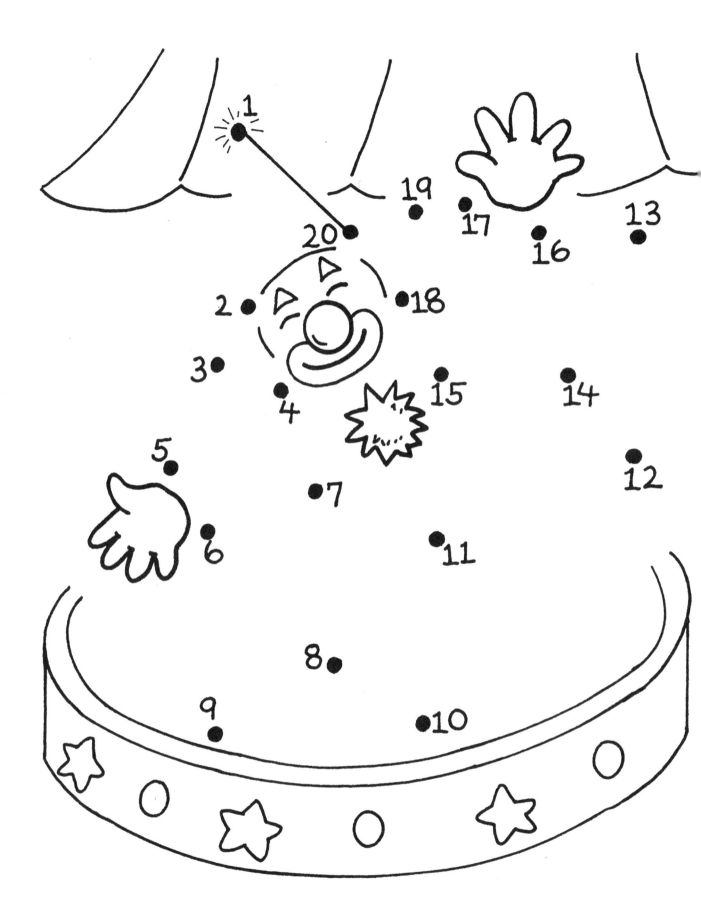

In the circus I give joy
And laughs to every girl and boy.

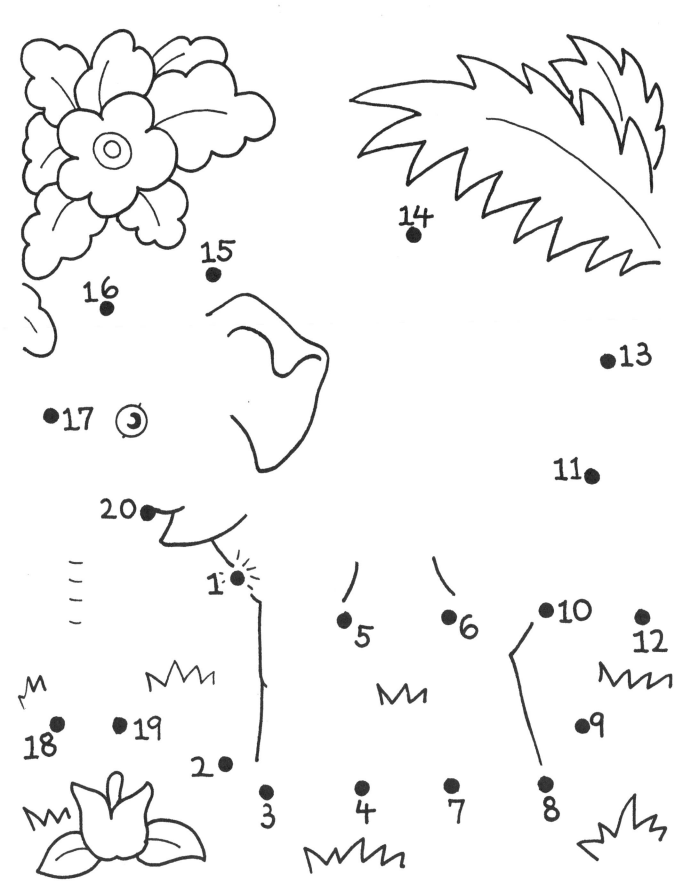

The largest animal on land,
I pick up things by nose, not hand.

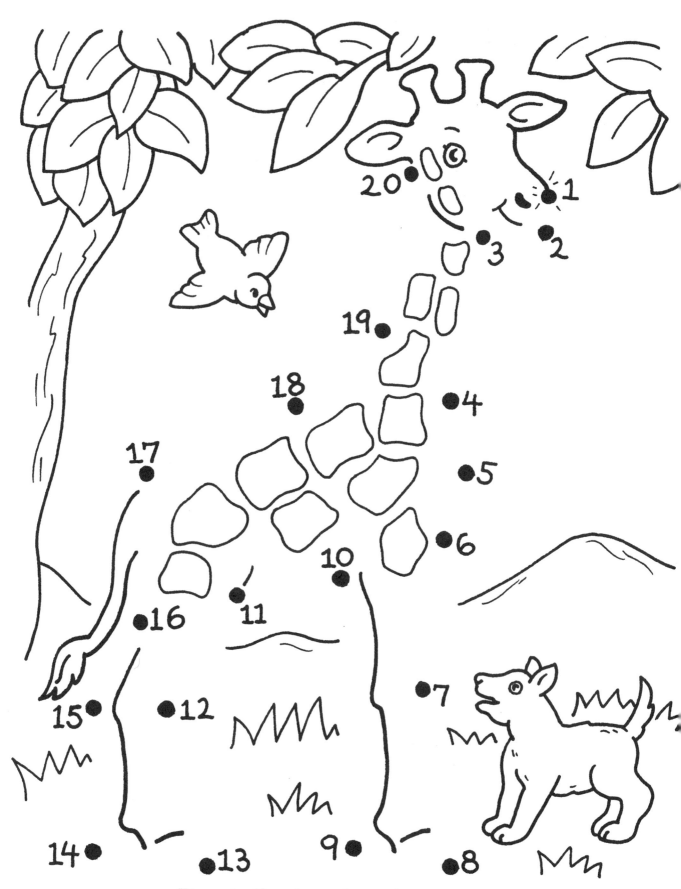

The tallest animal one sees,
He eats the leaves right off the trees!